A Visit with Vincent Van Gogh

Created and written by
SIMA LEVY

Illustrated by
Justin Morcillo

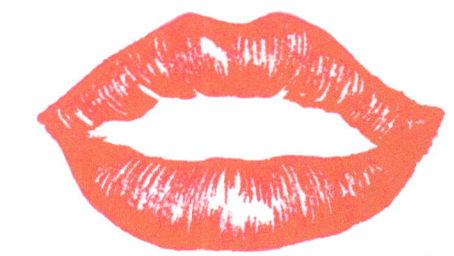

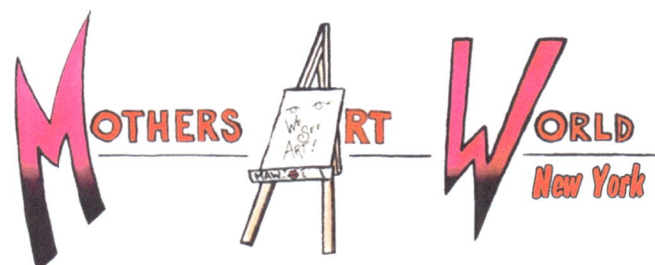

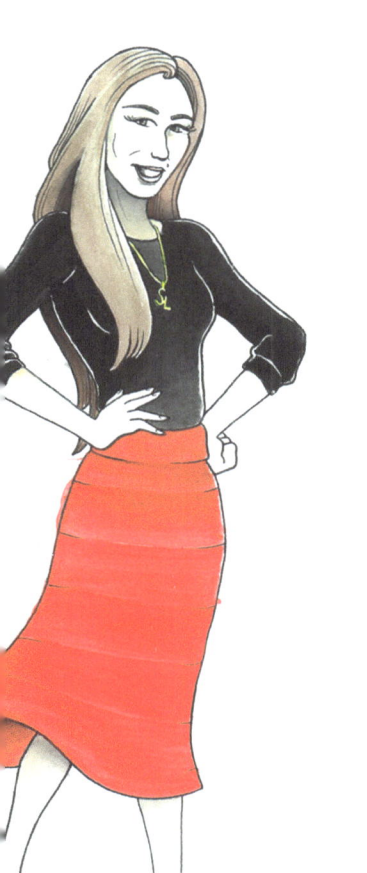

Van Gogh's Images Provided By
Collection/Bridgeman Art Library

ISBN: 1496165128
ISBN 13: 9781496165121

Published by
MAW Mothers Art World, Inc., New York
www.Mothersartworld.com

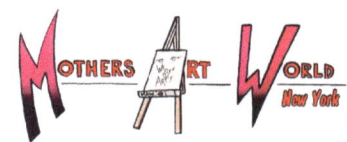

Summary:

Summary: Mays is a poet and artist in Ms. Simone's art appreciation class. The class is learning about the history and works of the Post-Impressionist artist Vincent van Gogh. As Mays gains knowledge about the style of Van Gogh, he realizes that he has a lot in common with the artist. Like Van Gogh, Mays uses his feelings to guide his painting and writing. But he has a dilemma: he doesn't know which to do first, compose his poem or illustrate. Mays's classmates Paris and Manet have a secret magic word that takes them to "The Land of Artists," and they decide to share their secret with Mays. They say "Wackadoey" three times and then – bingo! - they're in the Netherlands with Mr. Van Gogh. The artist teaches them to quickly capture their feelings of real life situations with heavy paint and thick brush strokes. He assures Mays that there is no set order when one is expressing oneself.

Back in art class, Mays decides to write his feelings about Van Gogh in a poem first, and then paints his own version of The Starry Night. The outcome is just right!

Read *A Visit with Vincent van Gogh* and you will experience a "Manet Day," learn to use your imagination to improve your art, and feel coo-cooey wackadoey. So what do you say?

Song: "Van Gogh's emotions." Lyrics by: Sima Levy.
Music by: Cory Dibona and Peter Scarlata.
Performed by: Peter Scarlata and Paris Levy

Song available on www.mothersartworld.com

I dedicate _A Visit with Vincent Van Gogh_ to all of my students who have inspired and touched my life.

Acknowledgements

First, I would like to thank my wonderful husband Jason for believing and supporting my vision. My loving children Jordan, Logan and Paris for inspiring me to write characters that reminds me of their personalities, for always wanting to listen to my ideas and share their opinions.

Thank you to my beautiful mom for always encouraging me to be the best that I could be and to follow my dreams.

Thank you to my delicious nieces and nephews for all the love and support. Love you more!!!

Much thanks Justin Morcillo for illustrating my vision as I see it! Justin, I love working with you and always proud of you!

Thank you Cohen's Medical Center, of the North Shore-LIJ Health System, for allowing me to share my knowledge and passion of art history, which can be intimidating to children. My goal is to eliminate that factor and teach in the way that is entertaining, informative and interactive.

Most importantly, I want to thank G-D for giving me the opportunity to give back to others. Thank you for your guidance as I am and we all are your children.

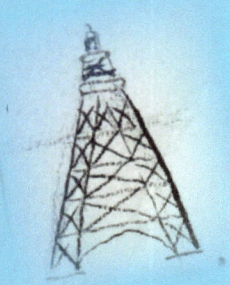

Buzz, buzz, buzz! The alarm is hounding.
"Good-bye, sweet dreams," it's sounding.

Time to get ready; adventures await.
So hurry up! Get moving! You can't be late!

"Paris," Mom calls, "don't forget your art supplies."
"I'm packing them now," she replies.

Off to school she goes, to join her friend Mays.
She can't wait to share with him, her imaginary ways!

 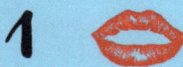

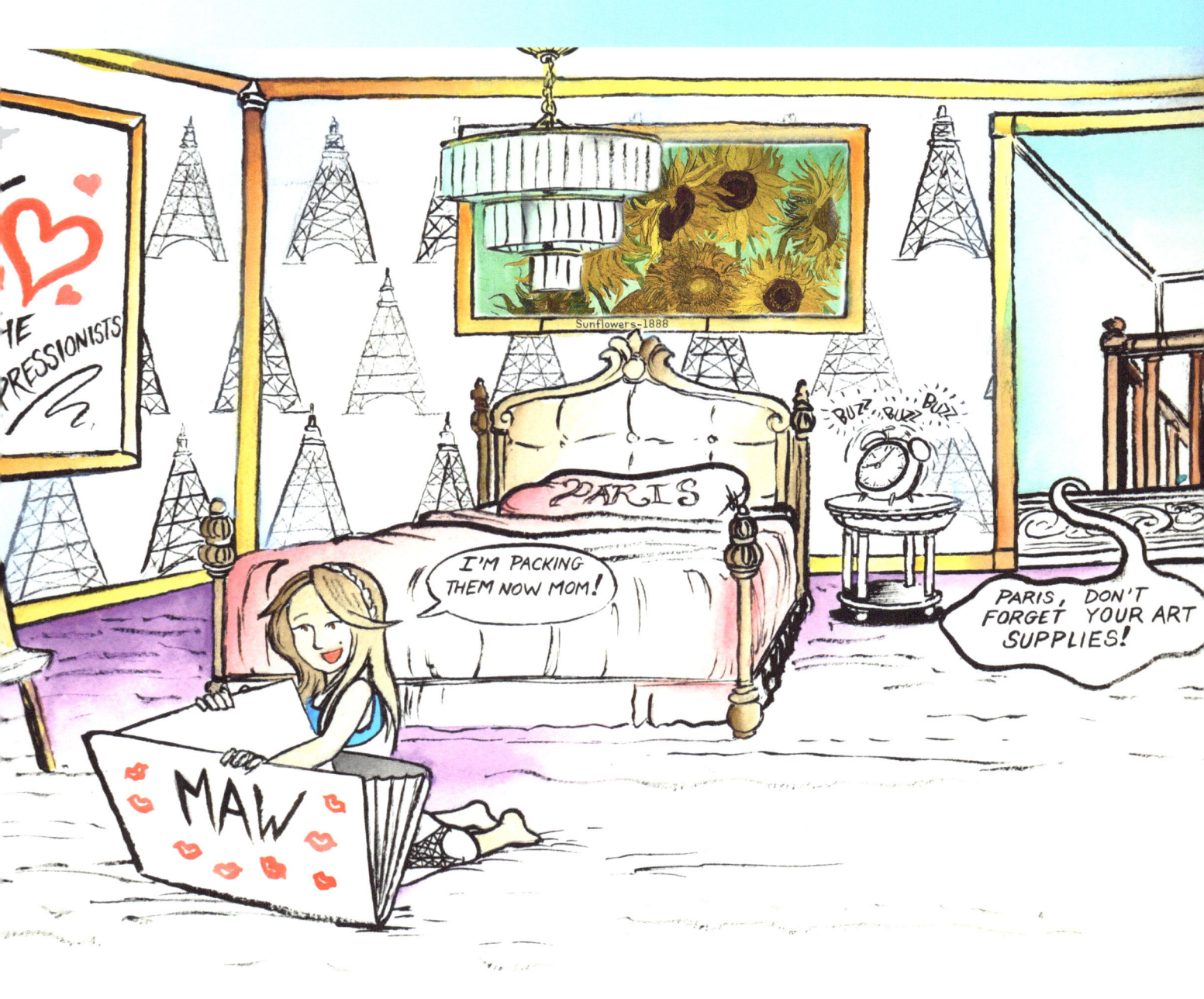

"Good morning, Mays," Paris greets, "I have great news for you."
"Hi, Paris," says Mays. "I have exciting news too.

But ladies first."
"Great," says Paris, "Cause I'm about to burst.

My mom told me that today she will teach
us about your favorite artist.
I'll give you a hint: He's Dutch, honest and quite modest."

"No way!" shouts Mays. "Is Ms. Simone's class about Van Gogh?"
Paris joins in her friend's excitement and says, "Bingo!"

"Well, Paris," exclaims Mays, "you too, will be happy with my news.
My parents are inviting you to join us this Sunday,
for an evening cruise.

We can watch the sky, just like Van Gogh,
For comets and shooting stars, as he did long ago."

Paris and Mays were happy as can be,
Skipping all the way to school with glee.

 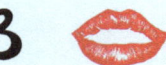

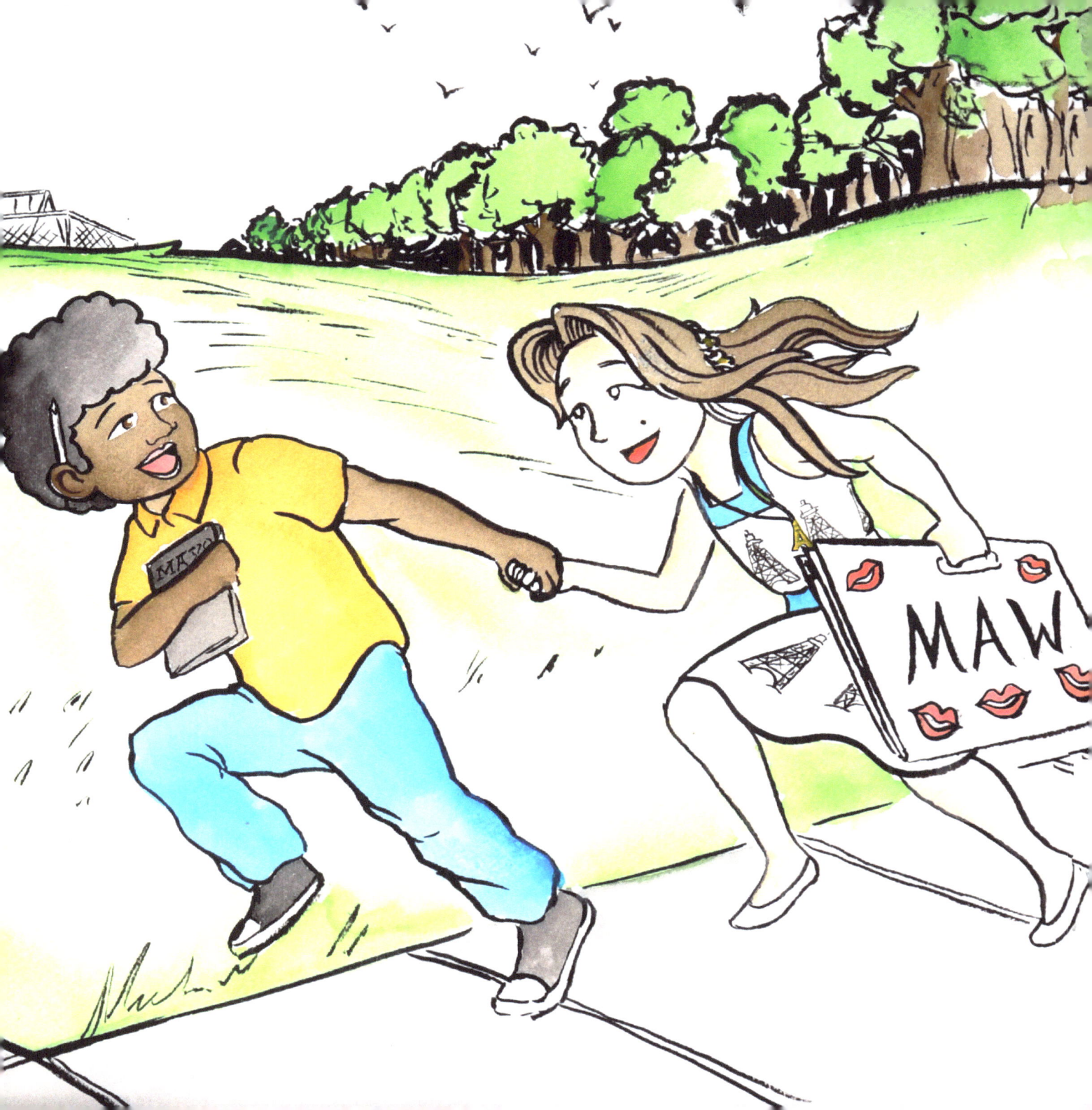

"Good morning class," greets Ms. Simone.
"Today we'll discuss the life and style of an painter once unknown.

Vincent van Gogh was a Dutch post-impressionist master,
But his talent went unrecognized; his life was a disaster.

His work is known for its rough beauty
Of real people, not the snooty.

Bold use of colors and swirly lines,
Influenced 20th-century art designs."

"What is post-impressionism?" asks Mays.
Ms. Simone replies, "It followed the impressionist phase.

Post impressionist artists can be recognized
For their use of vivid colors; their emotions emphasized.

Mays declares, "I guess I'm a post-impressionist poet,
I always write my feelings of a painting as I know it."

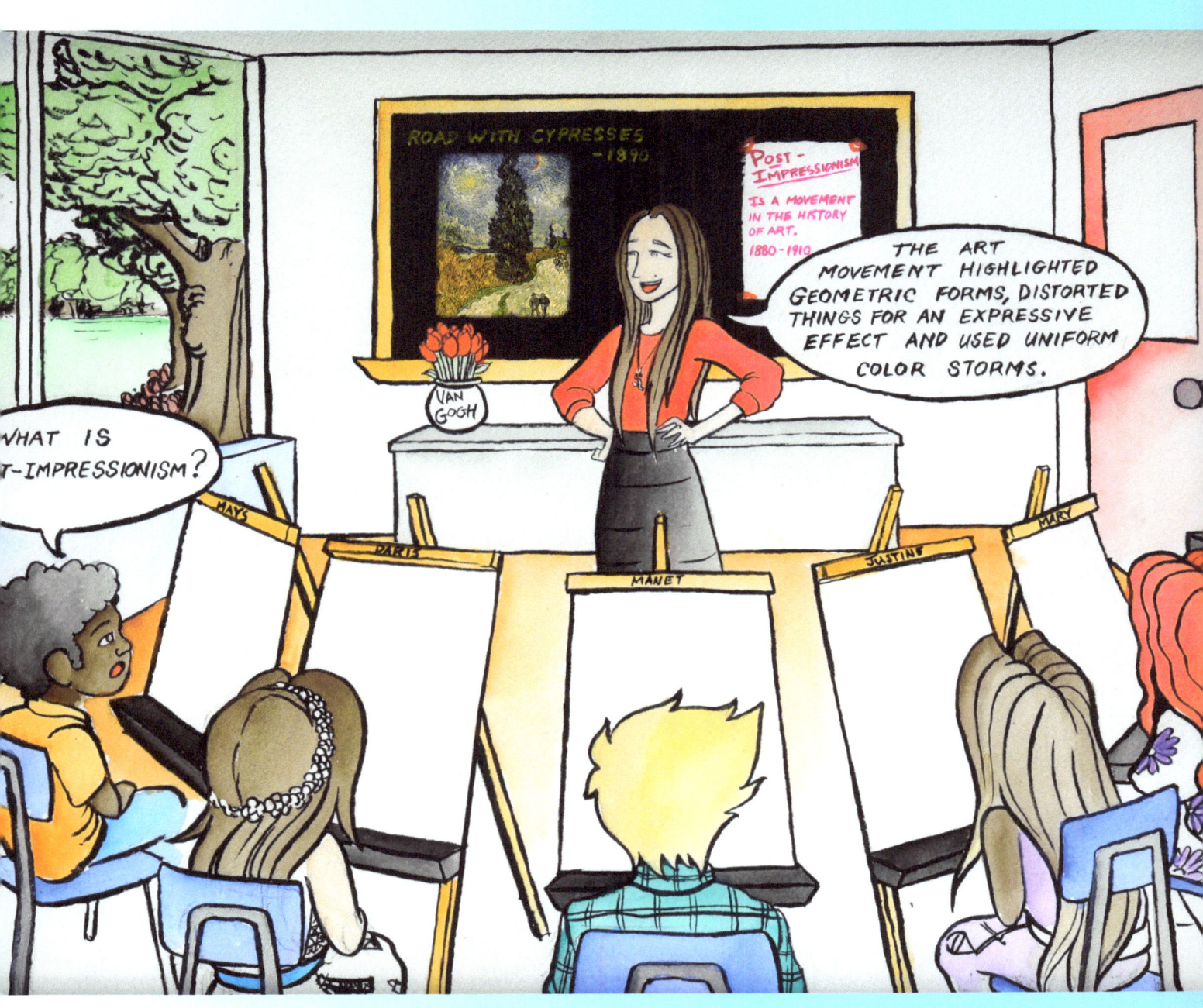

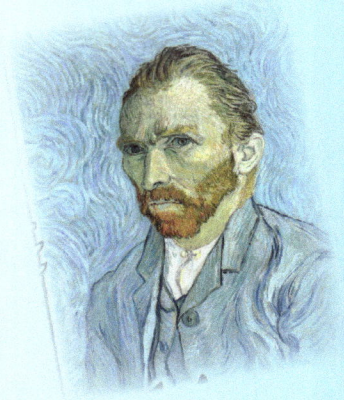

Ms. Simone lectures, "Van Gogh was born in 1853.
Expressing his emotions on canvas set him free.

He combined bold colors with geometric forms,
Producing works that were artistic color storms.

As a boy from the Netherlands, he wished to become a pastor.
Helping peasants is what he was after.

In the mining region, he began to draw.
Skillfully, he painted locals, and what he saw."

 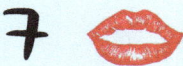

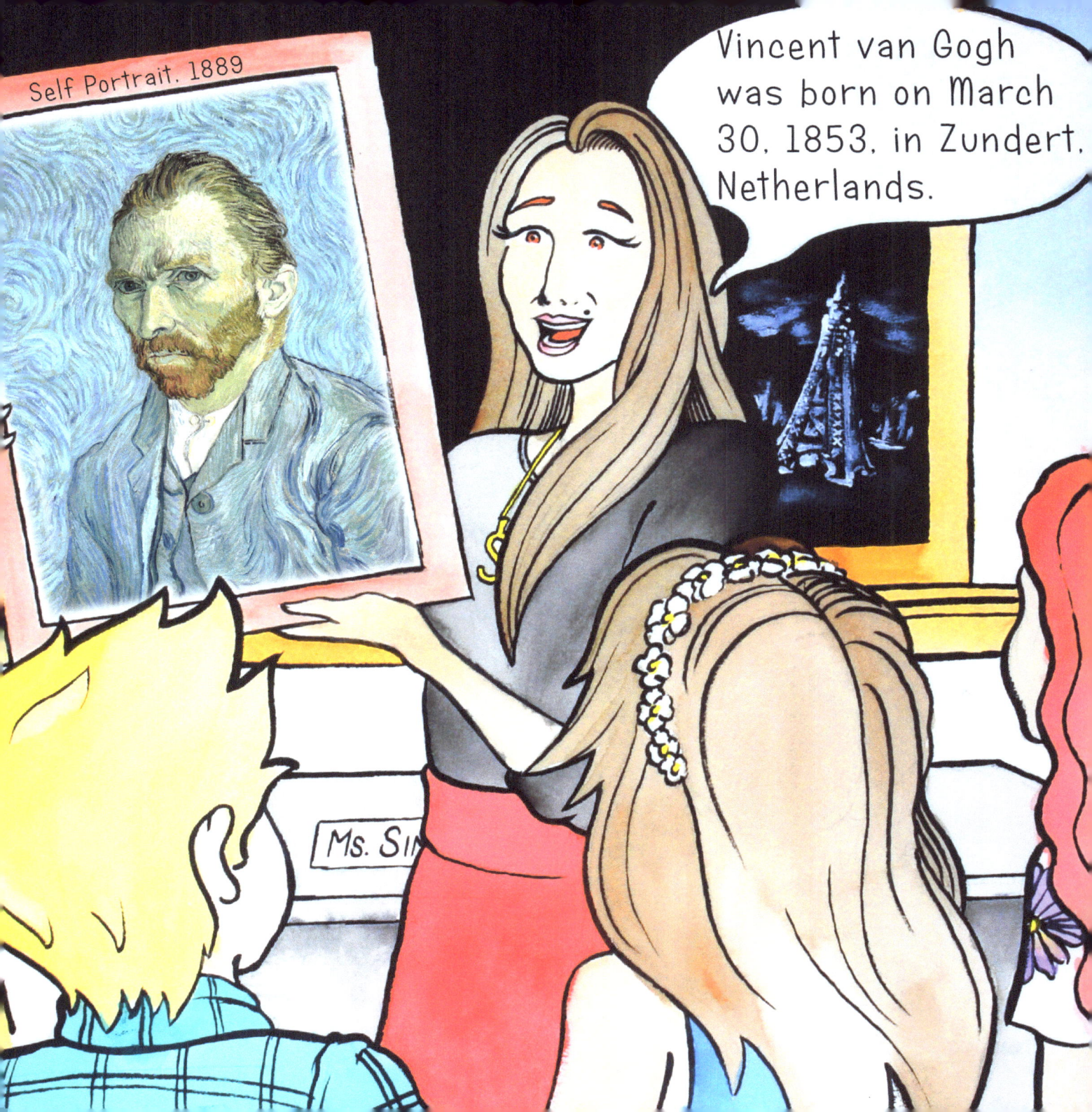

Paris exclaims, "Mr. Van Gogh was so nice!"

Mays adds, "Painting with meaning is wise."

"That's right," says Ms. Simone. "He proved to be among the art leaders

When he produced his first major painting, *The Potato Eaters*.

Self-portraits, landscapes and still lifes of different flowers,

Mr. Van Gogh had produced paintings of sky-high powers!"

Mays shares, "My favorite painting is *The Starry Night*.

I love how the stars shine, sparkly and bright."

Ms. Simone explains, "The painting is one of van Gogh's

Most famous and loved artworks, painted long ago.

In *The Starry Night*, the moon is a crescent,

The stars are bright and luminescent.

In Saint-Rémy, Vincent captured the sky late at night.

The village was asleep and the stars and moon were his delight."

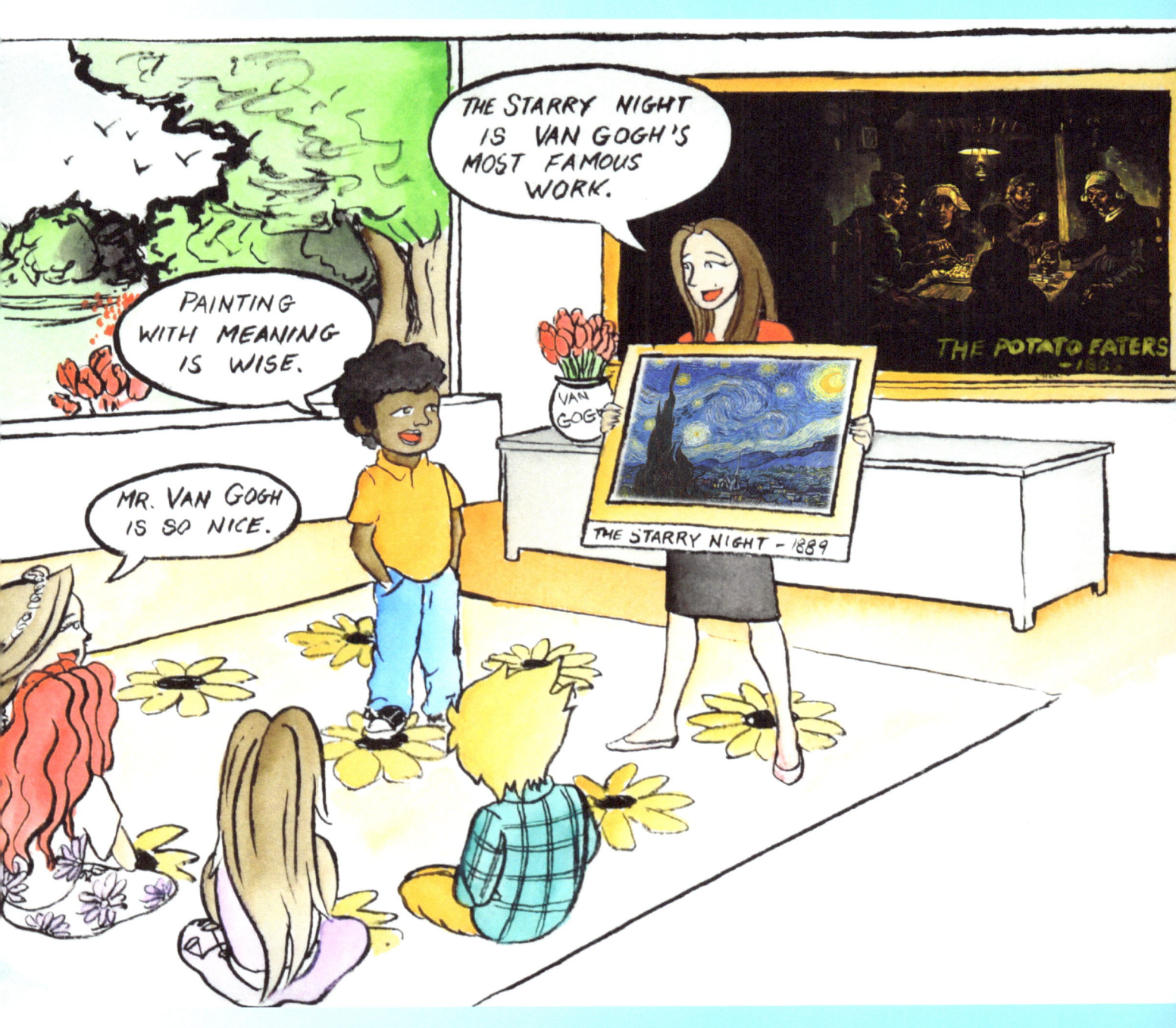

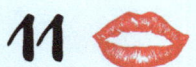

Mays is ready to compose his art;

Emulating Van Gogh: guided by his heart.

He wants his painting to be appealing;

To portray his thoughts, and capture what he's feeling.

Illustrating his poem first,

His technique is reversed.

Mays's Poetry:

A bouncing baby boy on March 30, 1853 was born.

Vincent van Gogh is the name that his parents chose.

He was a Dutch post-impressionist artist.

Painting with emotional honesty constant.

A young boy from the Netherlands, wishing to become a pastor;

Hoping to help peasants, from their unfortunate disaster.

Van Gogh's art entertains the world.

His lines are psychedelic and beautifully swirled!

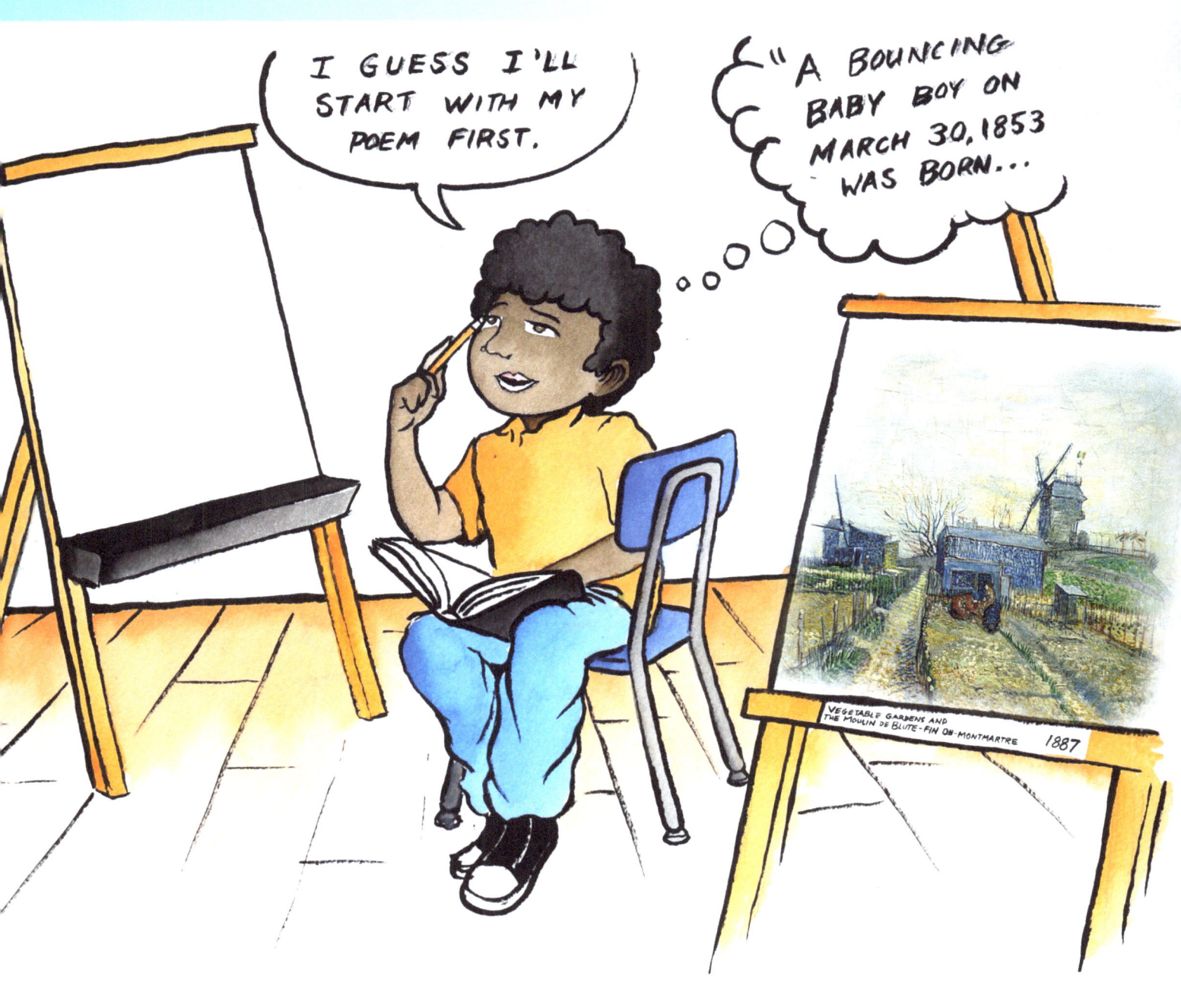

"Hey, Manet," says Paris, "lets take Mays to the land of artists.

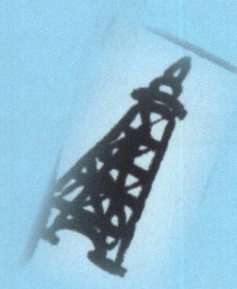

His favorite painter is Van Gogh.
Look how he's trying his hardest.

I would like for Mays to have a visit
with Van Gogh and spend the day."

Manet thinks for a moment, scratches
his head and finally says, "Okay."

Paris and Manet approach Mays and declare,
"Today is your lucky day."

Mays, curious, replies, "Oh, yeah?"

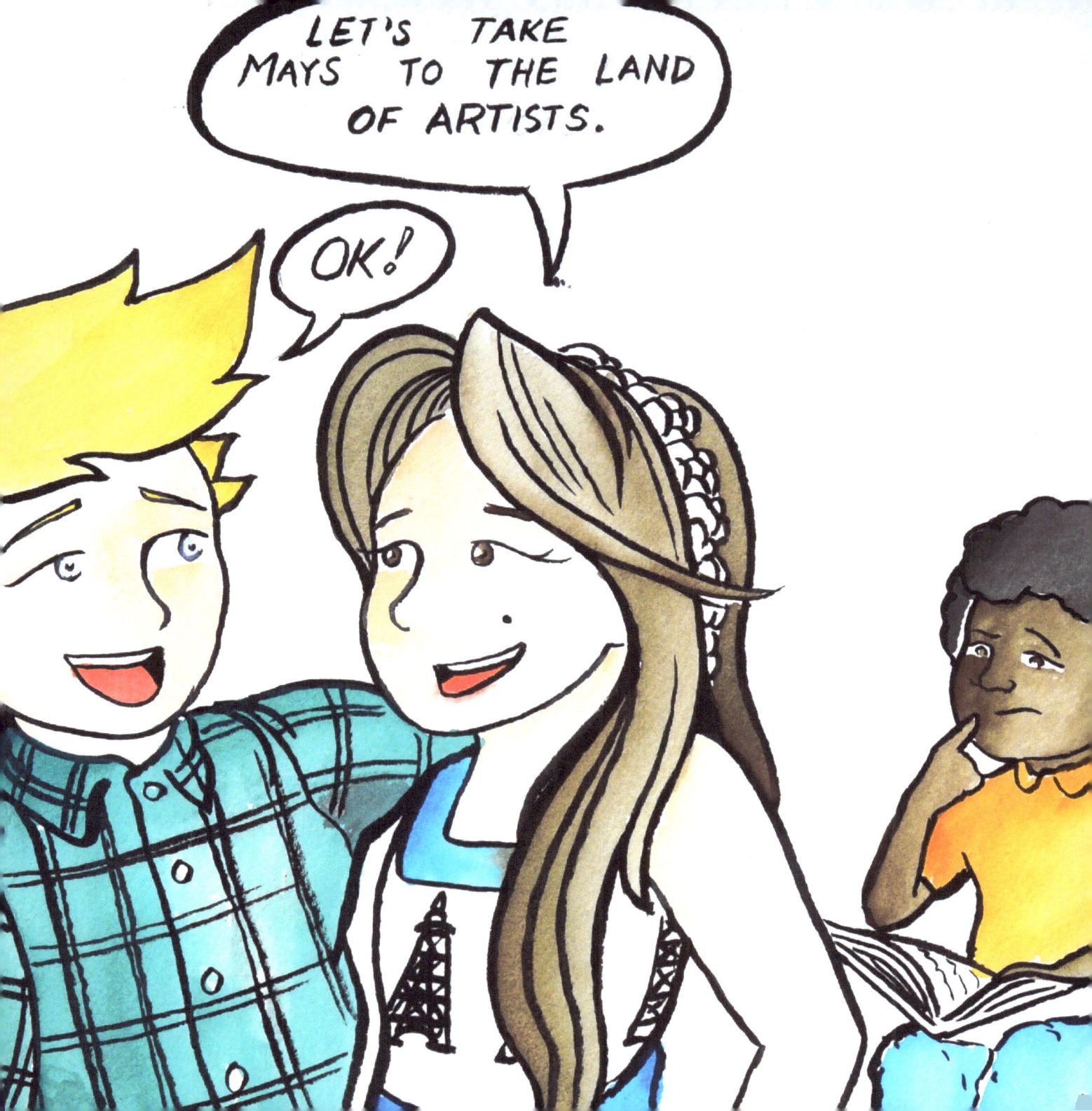

"Mays," says Manet, "close your eyes and do as I do.

In your imagination, you'll find the missing clue.

Being wackadoey will set you free.

Say it three times and you'll travel with me."

"Wackadoey! Wackadoey! Wackadoey!"

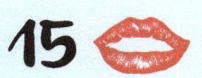

And away they blewy!

They dreamed of him and then - Bingo!

Standing right in front of them was Vincent Van Gogh!

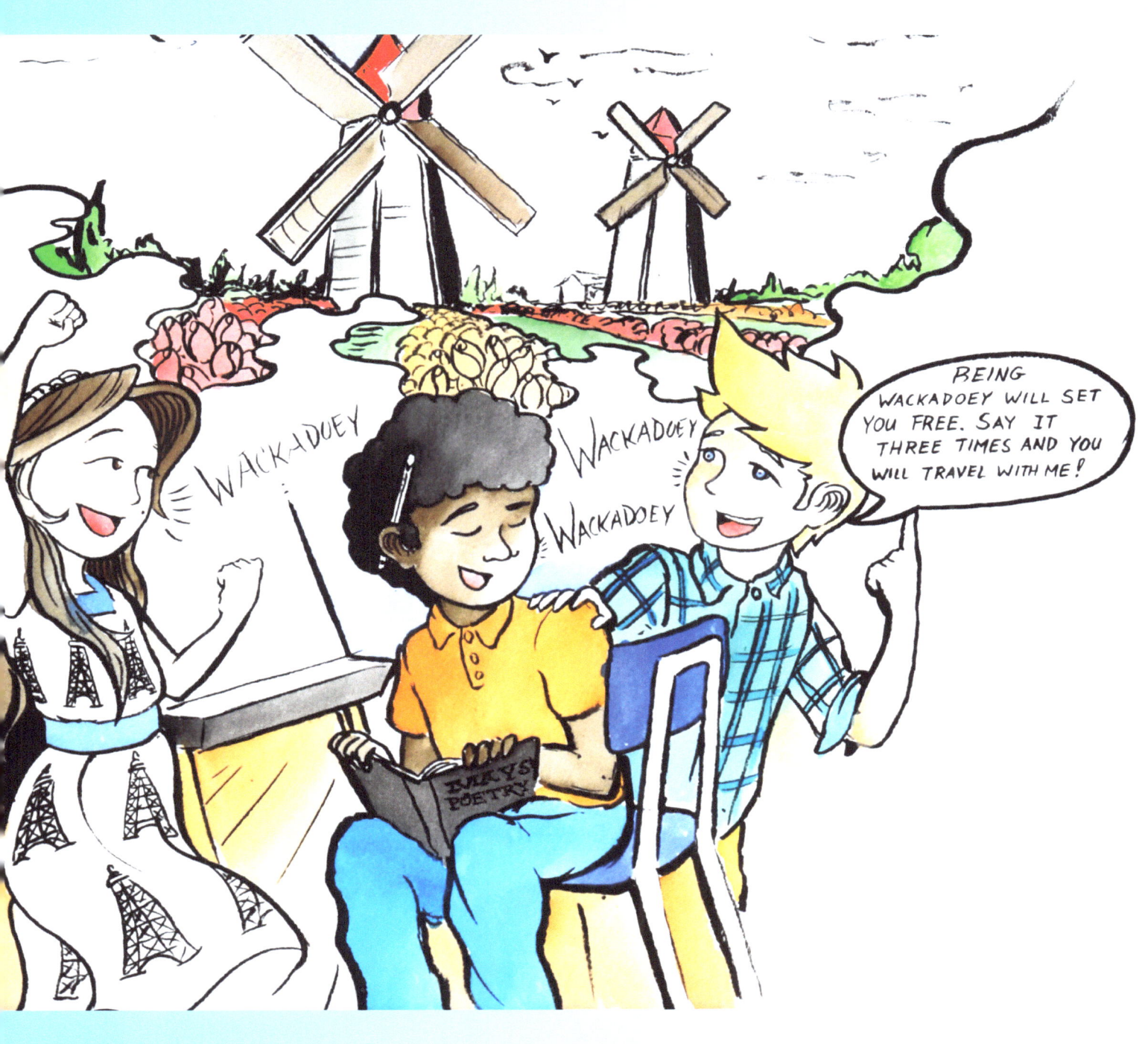

Van Gogh greets, "Welcome, children, to the Netherlands."

"Thank you," Mays replies, "it's as magical here as Never Never Land.

We came for a visit, Mr. Van Gogh.

Your style we wish to know.

How did you capture your feelings, in The Starry Night?

Like you, I write my thoughts down and it feels right.

But, how do I express them in my art?

Where should I start?"

Van Gogh answers, "Mays, I began to draw

People from local towns and what I saw.

The Potato Eaters became my first major piece of art.

My brother Theo was impressed and said, 'What a great start!'

My life's history is recorded and hopefully treasured."

Mays confirms, "From your "Dear Theo" letters, we are left pleasured.

17

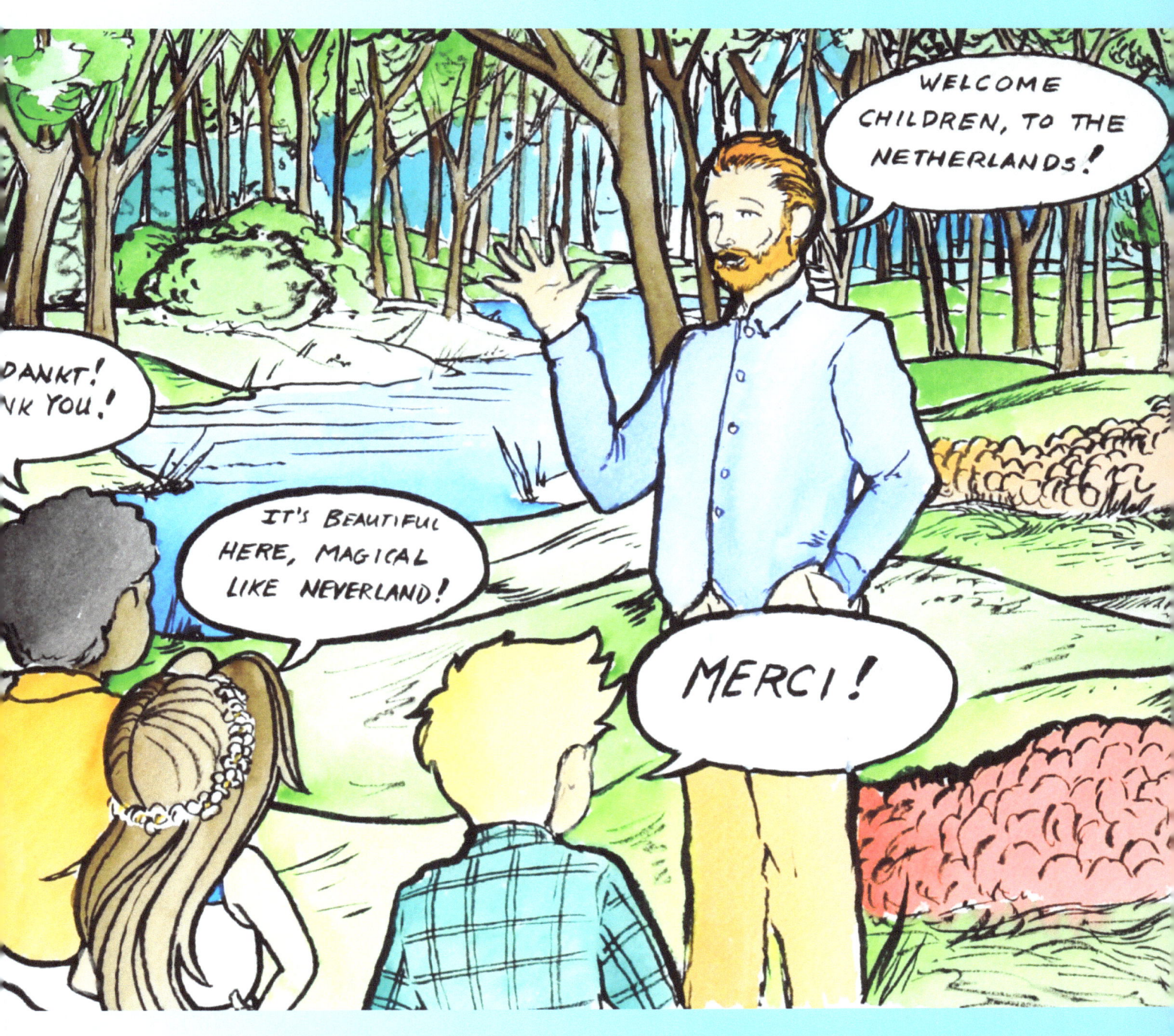

Do you write your feelings down, or paint them first?"

Van Gogh replies, "It depends on the moment; it's not rehearsed.

I'm amazed with what I see, and quickly paint what I feel.

Using swirly lines, bright vivid colors, and moments so real.

See Mays, there is no order to express expression.

If you're sensing creation and can paint the impression,

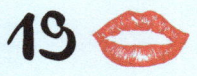

Then you should capture that first."

Mays confesses, "I did the reverse."

"That's absolutely fine," assures Van Gogh.

"Capture your feelings anyway you wish; don't stop, go!"

19

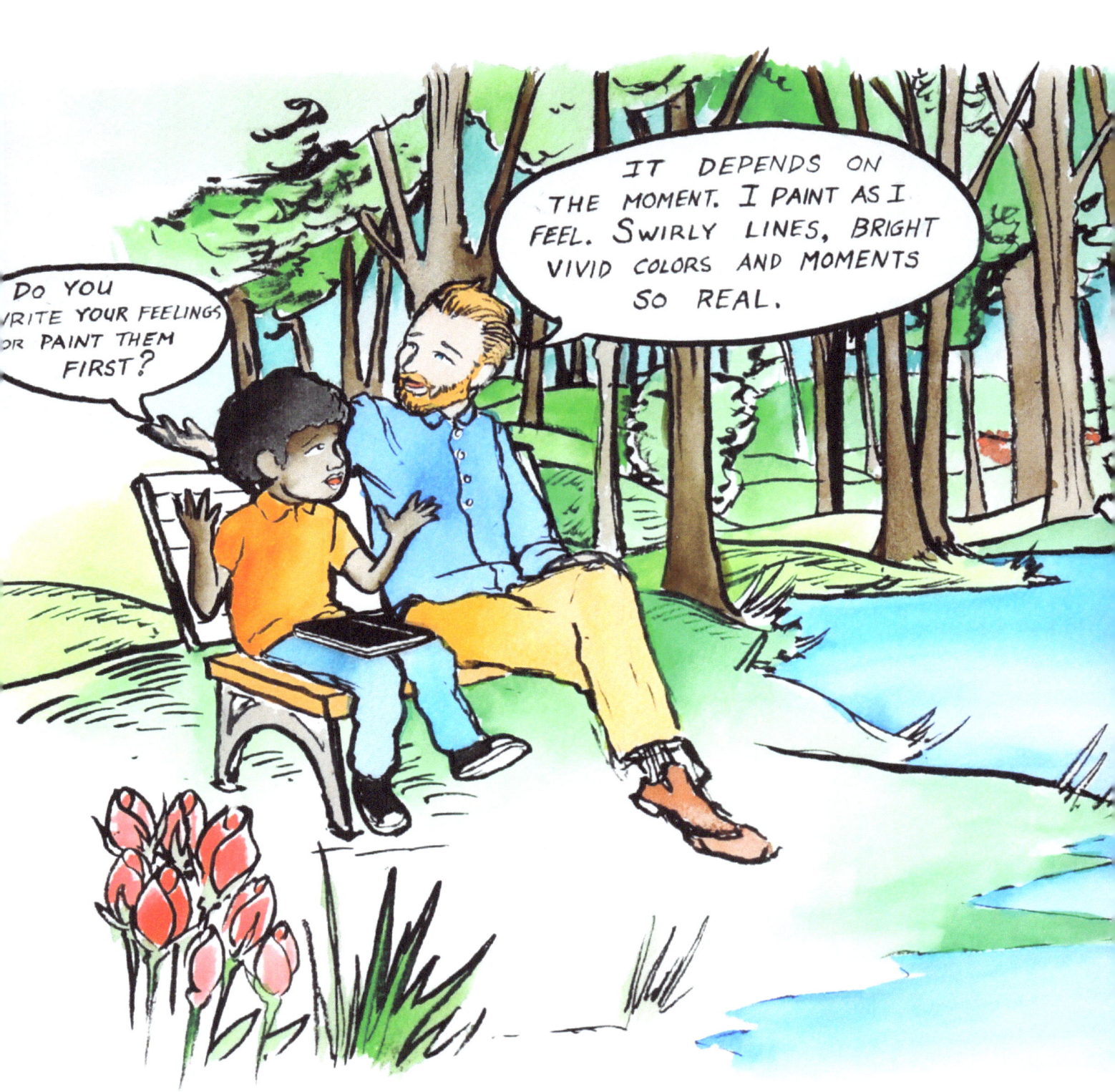

Paris asks, "Did you ever live in France?"

"Mon chéri, I lived in the city of your name, the city of romance.

In Paris, I painted with thick bold brushstrokes,

Outlining in black, flowers, self-portraits and common folks.

Gauguin and I moved to Arles, South of France.

We changed our style and took a chance.

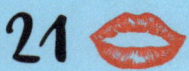 Painting outdoors as Impressionists.

The sun and the land became my interests.

I began producing sunflowers in bloom.

Gauguin was my mentor, till we argued and boom!"

Paris shares, "Your Sunflowers painting is hanging on my wall.

It's a copy, because the original is expensive, after all."

"Good to know, mademoiselle," states Van Gogh.

"I didn't make lots of money years ago."

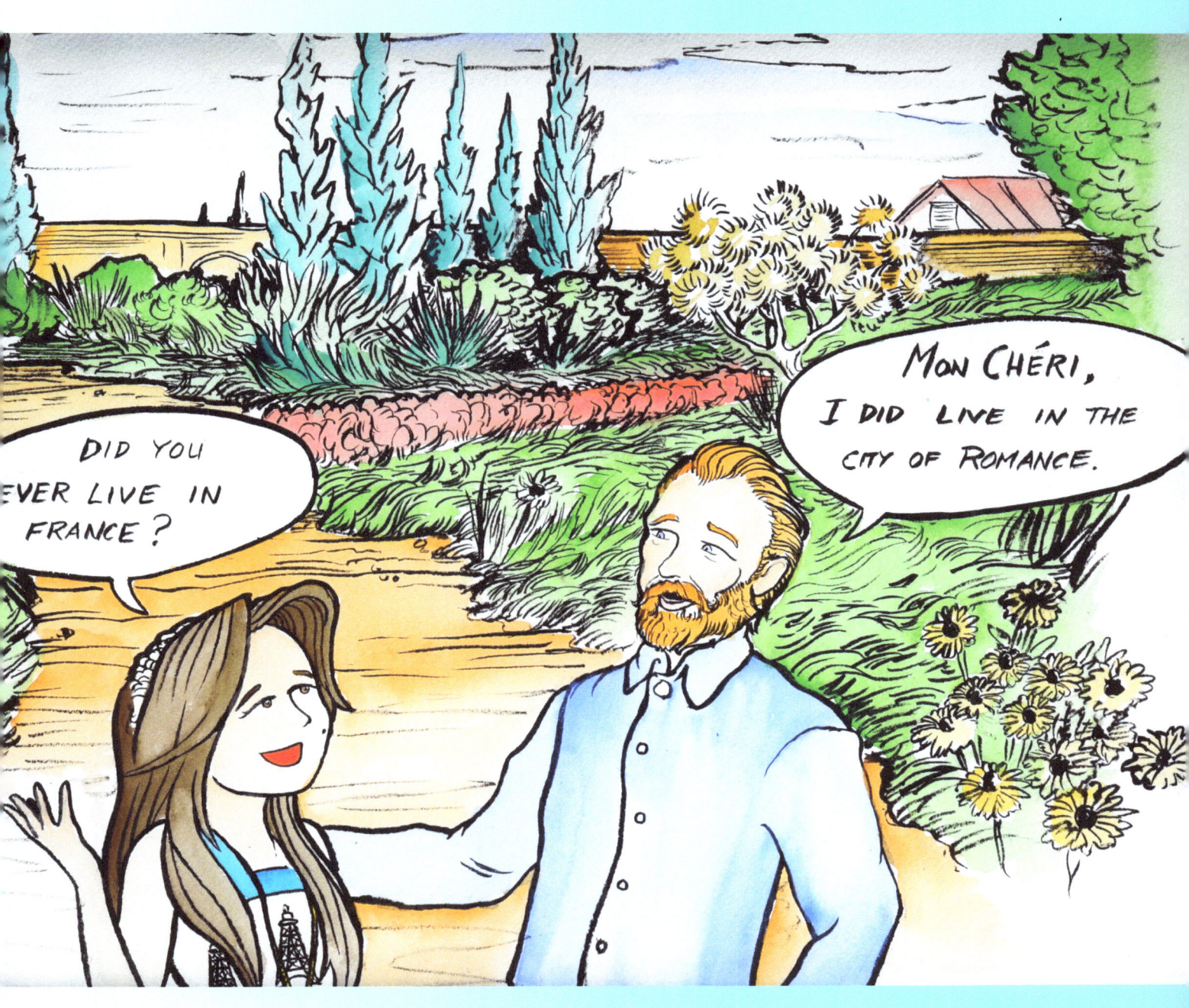

Mays says, "Mr. Van Gogh, you are so famous today.

Your art is studied and emulated every day!

My favorite painting of yours is *The Starry Night*.

What were you feeling as you painted the sight?"

Van Gogh begins, "The moon was a crescent,

The stars were bright, yellow, and luminescent.

I felt the energy of the sky,

I painted the scene as a spy.

With swirled lines, I captured the energy of the night.

Painting the moon and stars, happy and bright."

Mays agrees: "I can see the movements in the sky.

My eyes keep moving, following the curves, not knowing why.

The village you kept asleep and in the dark.

The sky was your friend, and the focus mark."

"Correct! You are expressive just like me," Van Gogh says proudly.

"Sensitive too," adds Mays, and they both laugh loudly!

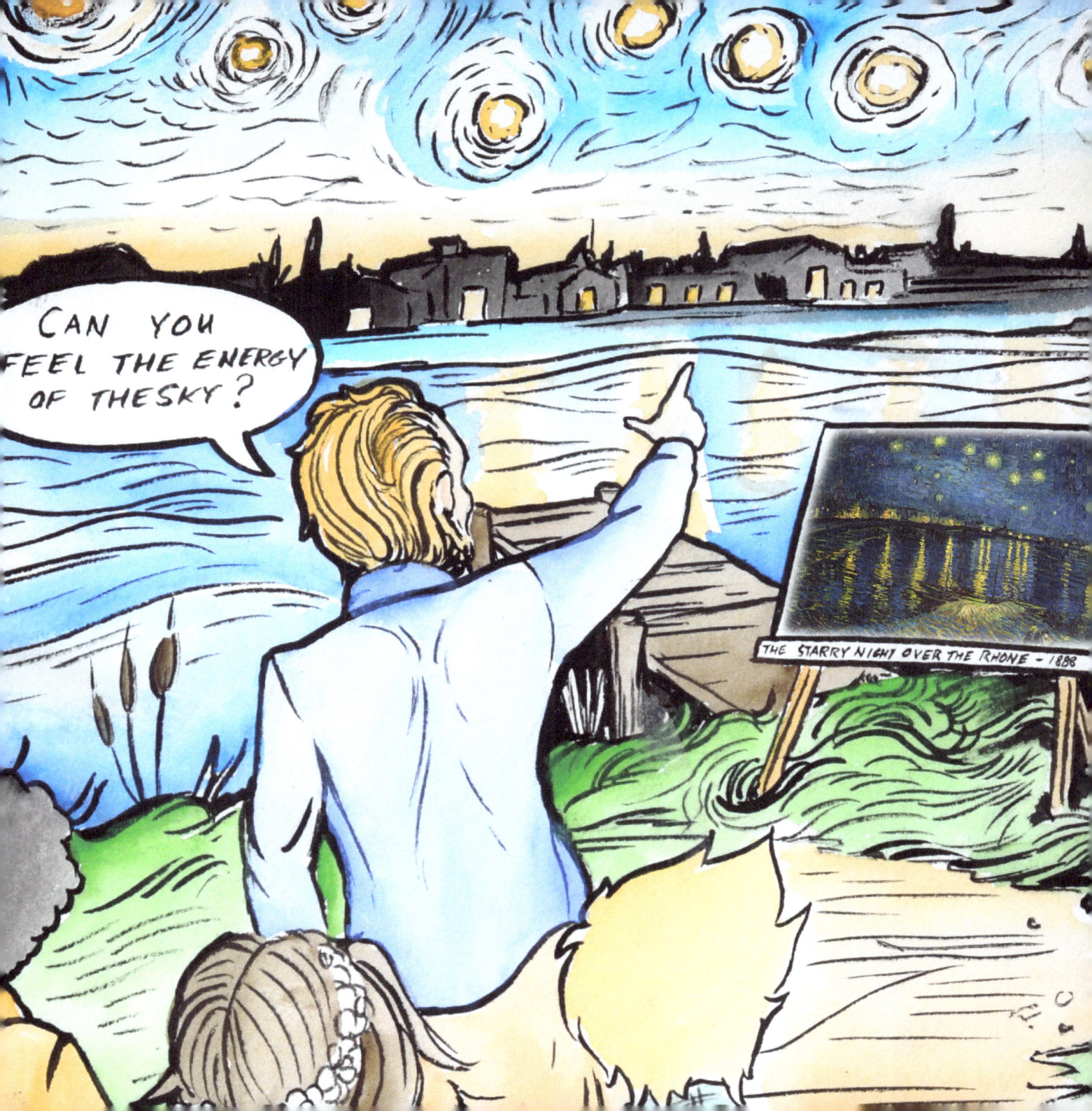

Justine has just finished her painting of "Irises."

Realizing that her friends are sleepy and soon will need mattresses.

She whispers in Mary's ear, "What's wrong with Paris, Mays, and Manet?

Their minds seem to be so far away."

Paris wakes up first and explains, "We were in the land of the artists."

"I don't understand," Justine states. "What land of artists?"

Paris replies, "I'm sure you will find out one day.

But art class is about to end and they cannot stay."

"Earth to Mays and Manet," whispers Justine,

"Come back! Art class is ending in fifteen."

"Au revoir," they say, "we have to head west.

Thanks, Mr. Van Gogh, you're the best!"

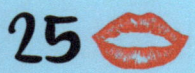

25

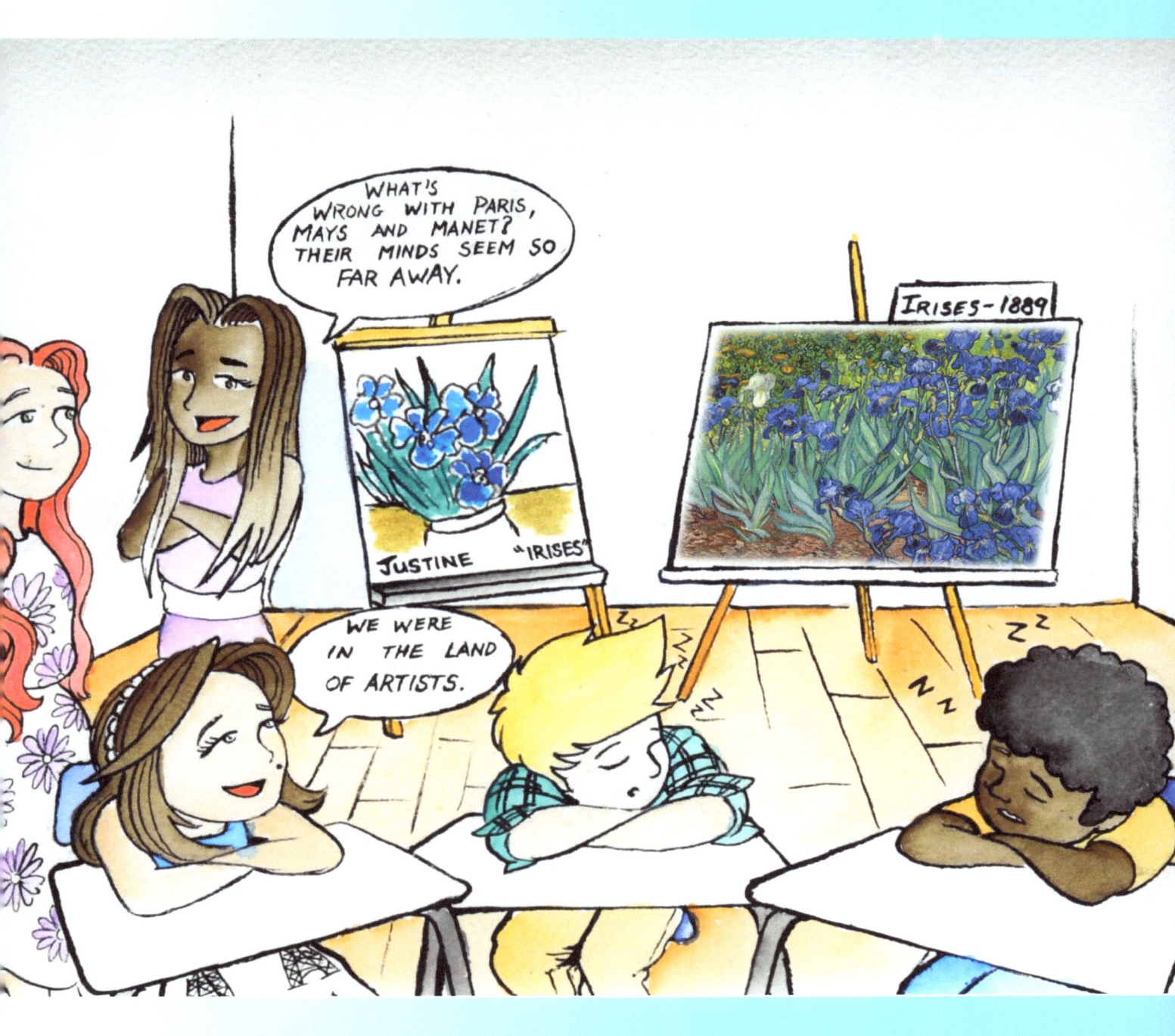

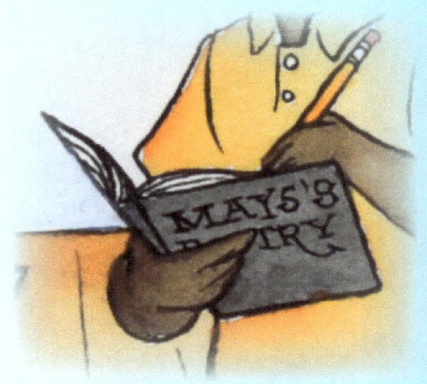

Mays recalls his visit and it shows in his smile.

His emotions are simply running wild.

He thinks he should relax and write them down first.

"Van Gogh was right," says Mays. "It's not rehearsed!"

Ms. Simone says, "Your feelings are alive, I can feel your joy.

Write, write, before the moment is lost; oh boy!"

 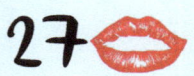

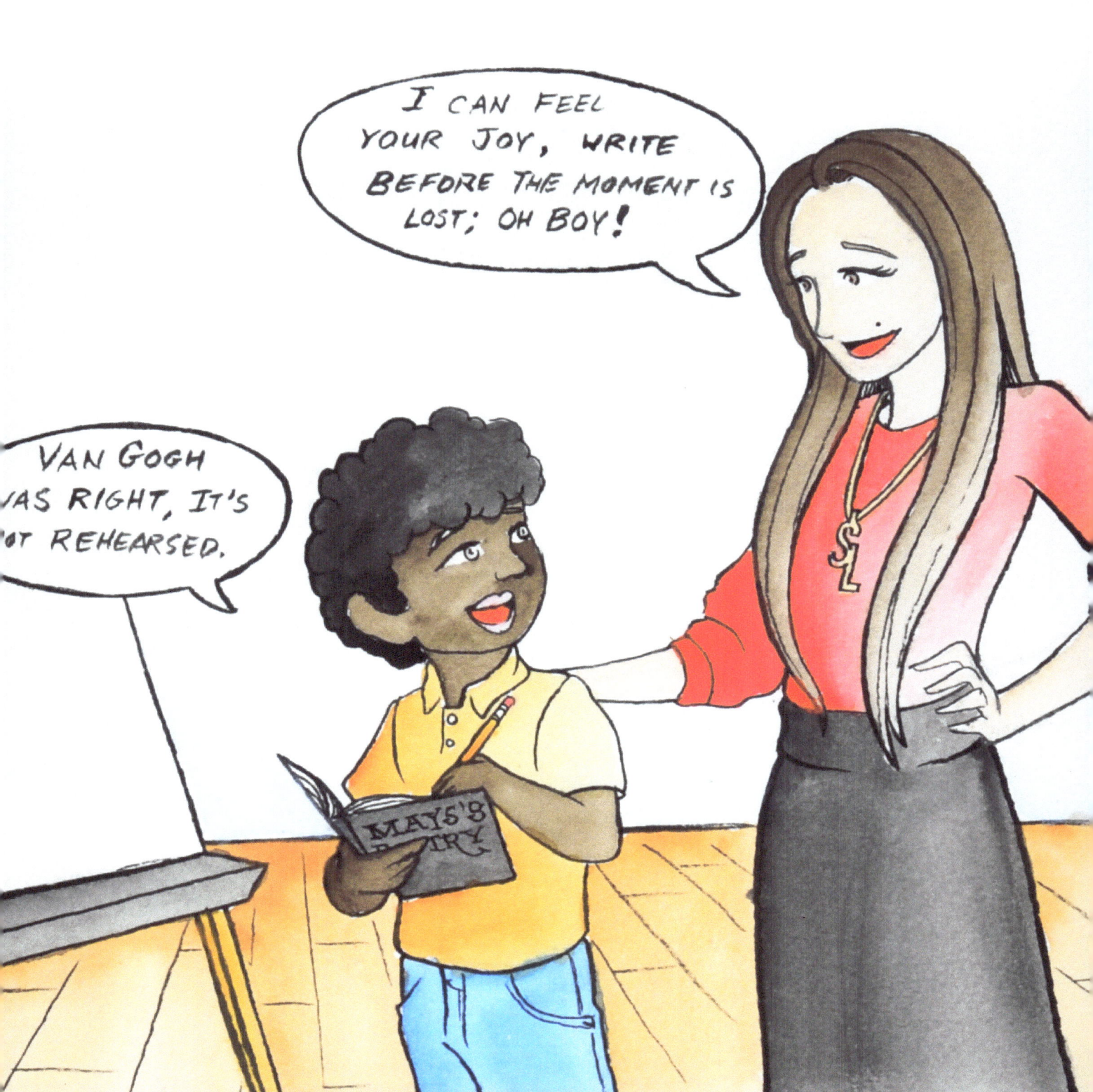

Paris declares, "What a beautiful night!
Thanks for inviting my family.

I can feel the energy of the sky here, so easily."

"Its our pleasure," says Mays.
"Cruises makes me feel calm and inspired.

I can illustrate the liveliness of the sky,
without getting tired!"

"I can see that," says Paris. "Please continue.

Paint away. I can't wait to get a preview!"

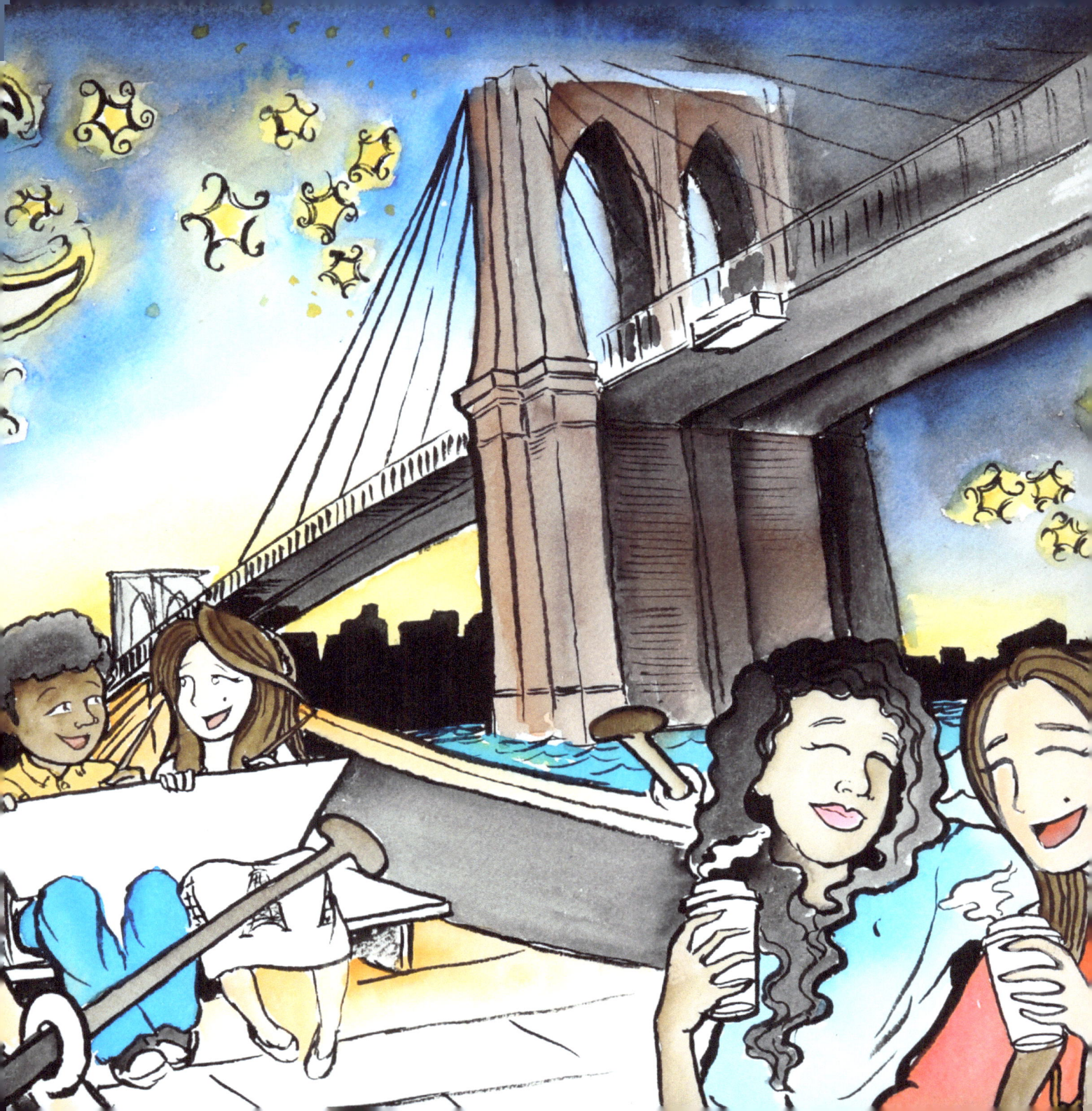

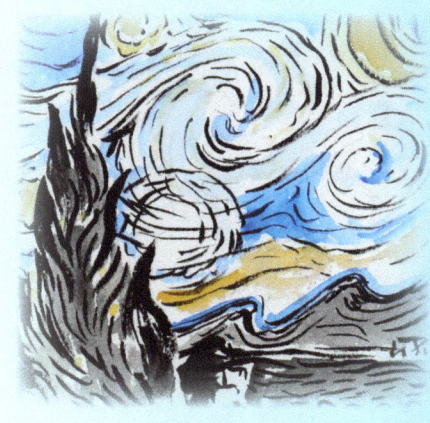

Mays enters art class with a confident stride,

A poem in one hand, a painting in the other,
and a smile of pride!

Ms. Simone says, "Mays, I'm impressed
with your painting and poetry.

Both are beautiful ...and perfectly WACKADOEY!"

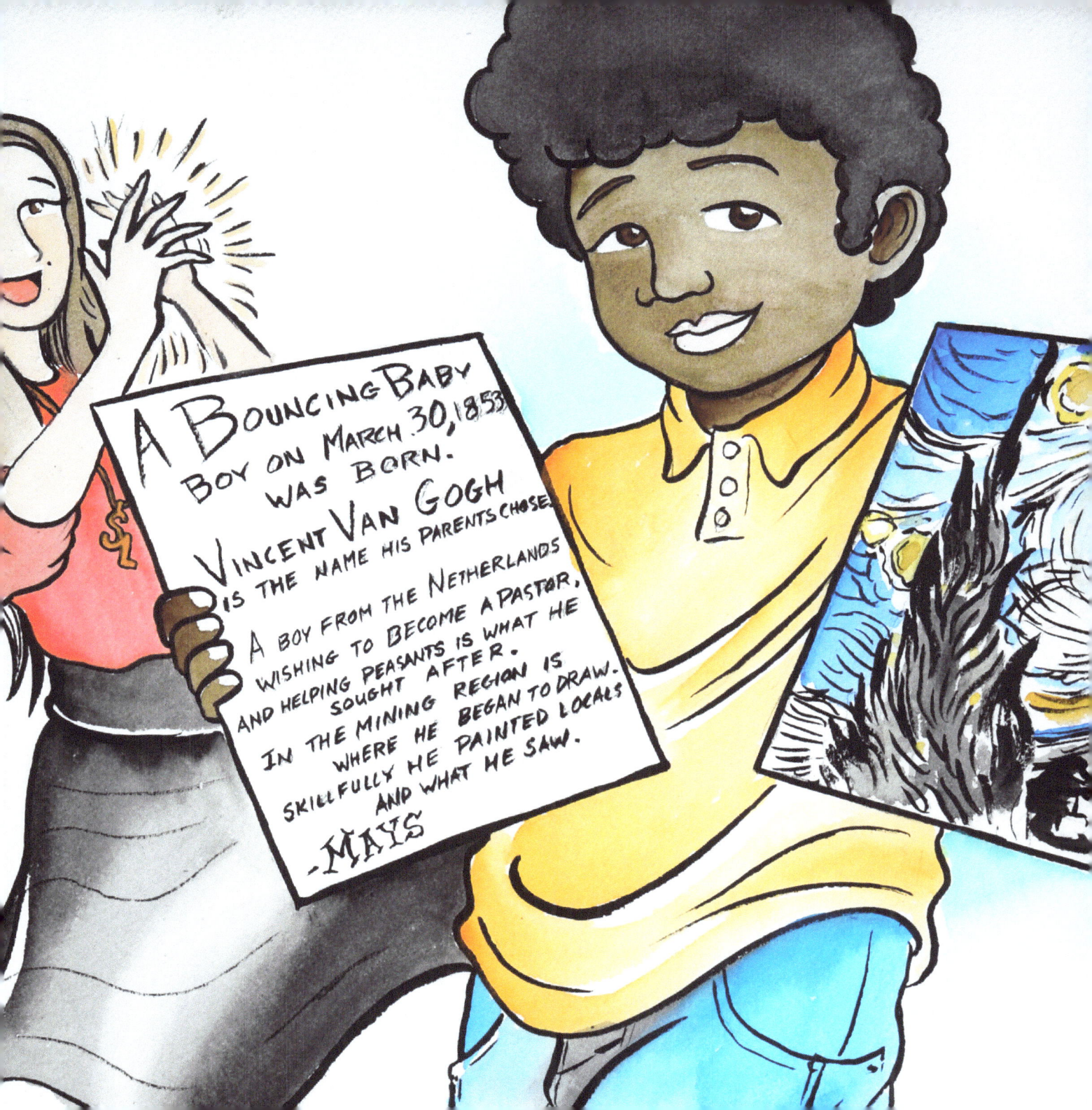

About the Author

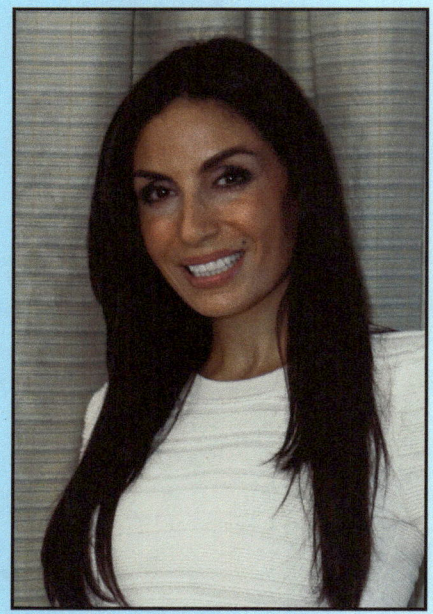

I founded Mothers Art World to give all children access to the world of art. Art is an essential part of every child's development, helping them use both sides of their brain while embracing expression and imagination to create something wonderful. Studying art helps children understand the connections, shapes, colors and ideas that exist in every artist's work.

Teaching art history to children in a way that encourages their creativity and interest rather than being intimidating (or boring!) is the inspiration behind Mothers Art World's *Meet the Artist Series*.

I was born in Tel Aviv, Israel and moved with my family to New York when I was 8. The year before, my brother Donny had died of a brain tumor at the age of 17. His premature death had a profound affect on me. As a child

I became passionate about giving back to the world through charitable works and education. What I was unable to do as a child, I have been able to begin to accomplish as an adult. The *Meet the Artist Series* is the first step in making those dreams become reality.

I introduced MAW art appreciation to Cohen's Medical Center. The children give me joy, love and inspiration. I co-run, train and teach art appreciation at the Schechter Day School of Nassau County.

Ms. Simone is a reflection of how I teach and display art throughout the classroom. I want children to be inspired by art history in a way that encourages them to begin their own creations. All children (and adults too!) need to experience being told 'great job,' 'you can do it', and 'aren't you awesome?' Art gives children just that opportunity to express, learn and feel accomplishment.

Charitable work remains a central part of my life. I'm a member of the Women's Health Committee at Katz Women's Hospital, a member of the Autism Committee, involved at Sunrise Day Camp, a camp dedicated to children with cancer and a member of UJA's Connection.

I'm a mother, wife, teacher, writer and creator. I enjoy spending time with my husband Jason and children Jordan, Logan and Paris, all of whom have contributed to the development of the *Meet the Artist Series*. Most evenings, I can be found sitting in front of the computer dreaming about the next adventure for Ms. Simone, Paris, Manet and the rest of the gang.

Other books in the *Meet the Artist Series*: *A Day with Degas*, *A Rendezvous with Renoir* and *A Moment with Monet*.

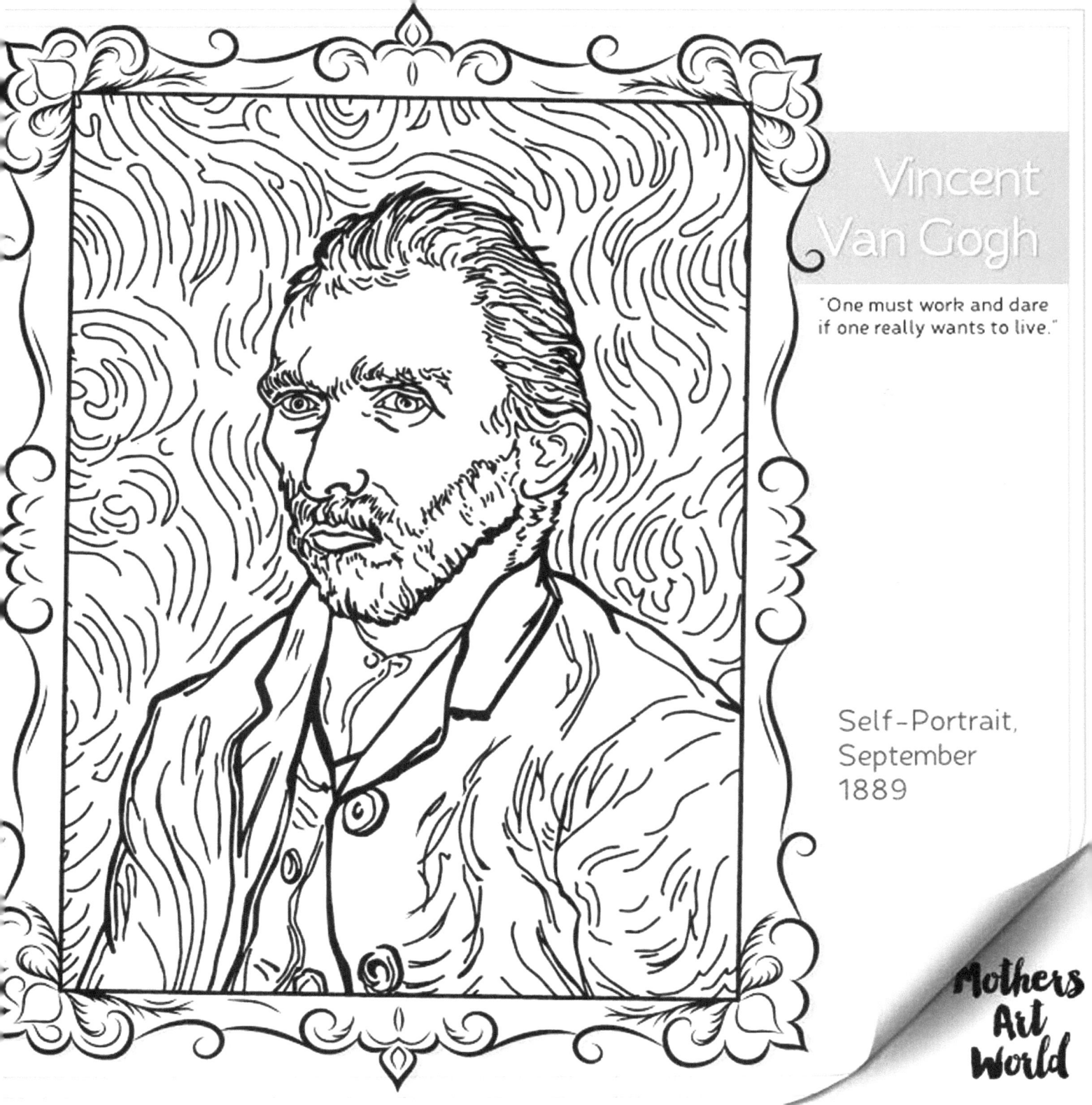

Vincent Van Gogh

"One must work and dare if one really wants to live."

Self-Portrait, September 1889

Mothers Art World

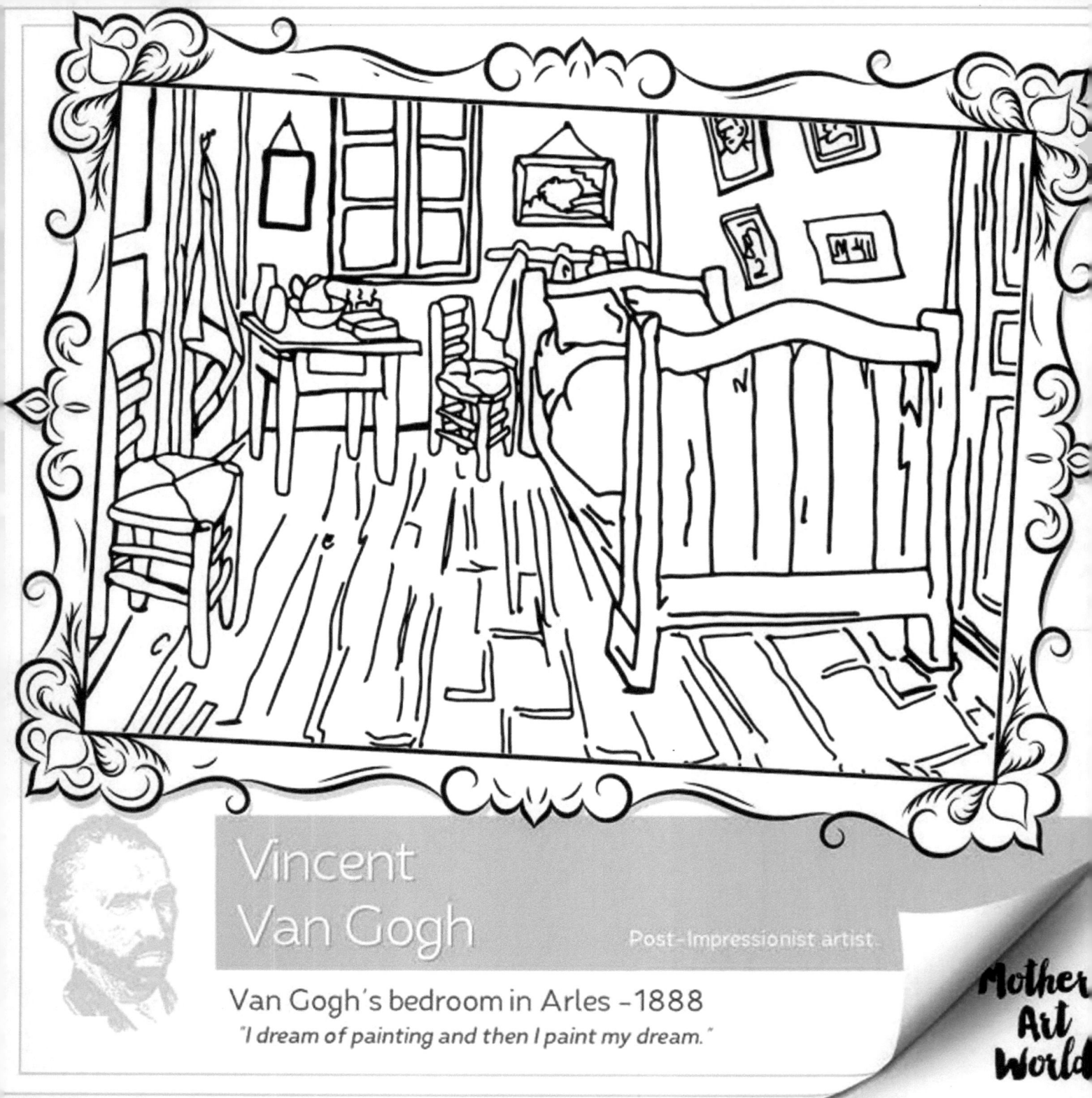

Vincent Van Gogh

Post-Impressionist artist.

Van Gogh's bedroom in Arles –1888

"I dream of painting and then I paint my dream."

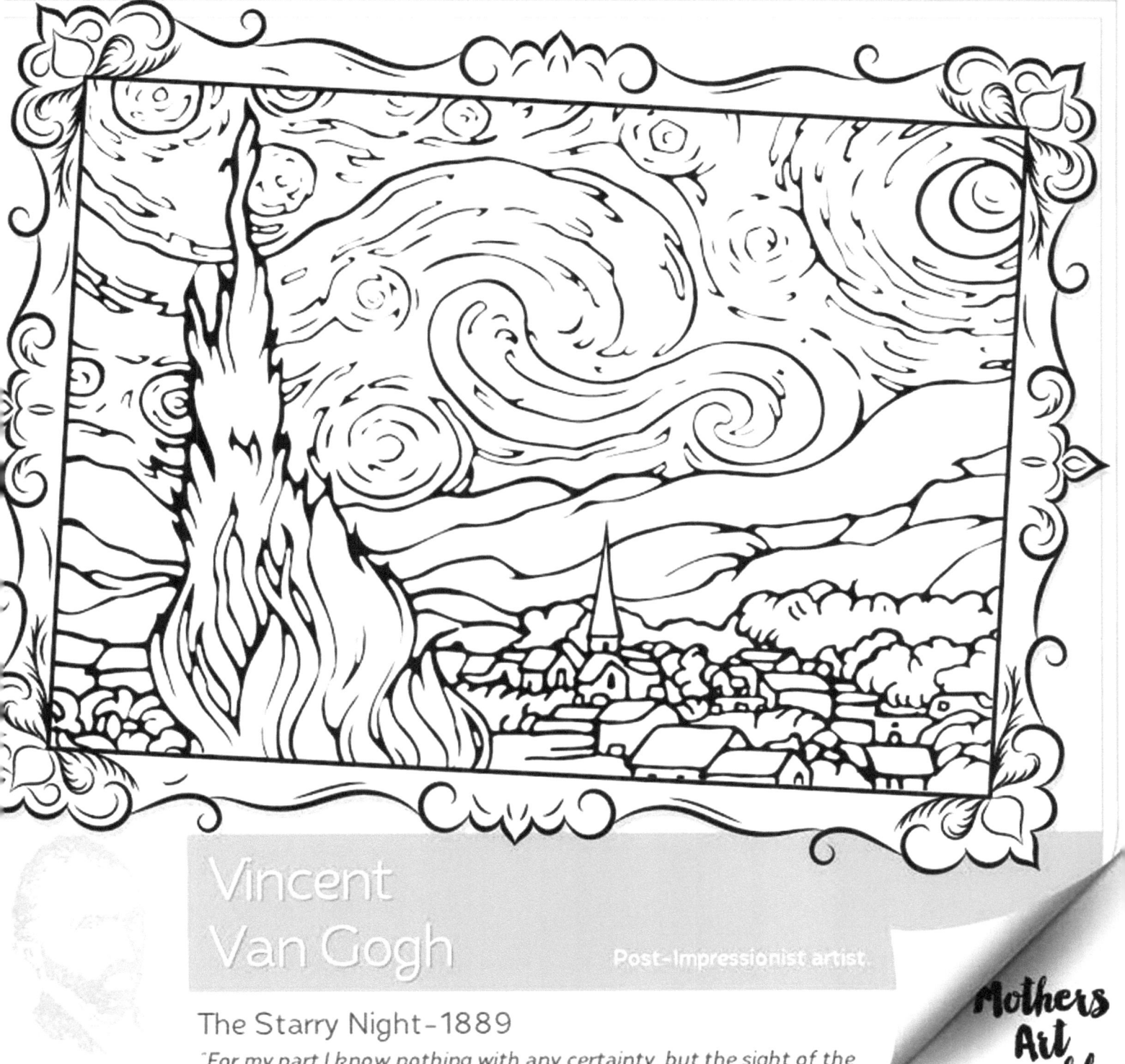

Vincent Van Gogh

Post-Impressionist artist.

The Starry Night-1889

"For my part I know nothing with any certainty, but the sight of the stars makes me dream."

Mothers Art World

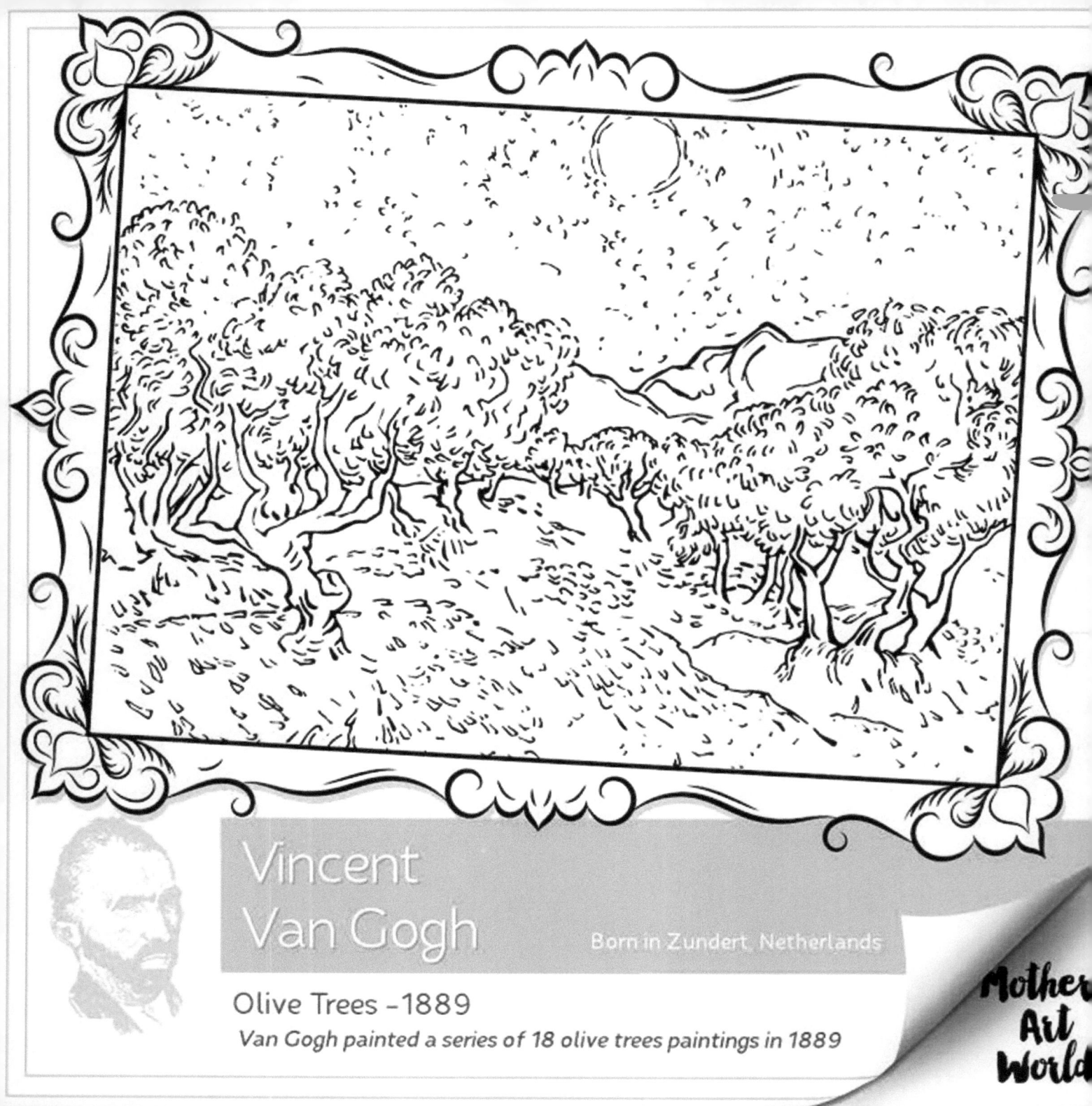

Vincent
Van Gogh

Born in Zundert, Netherlands

Olive Trees –1889

Van Gogh painted a series of 18 olive trees paintings in 1889

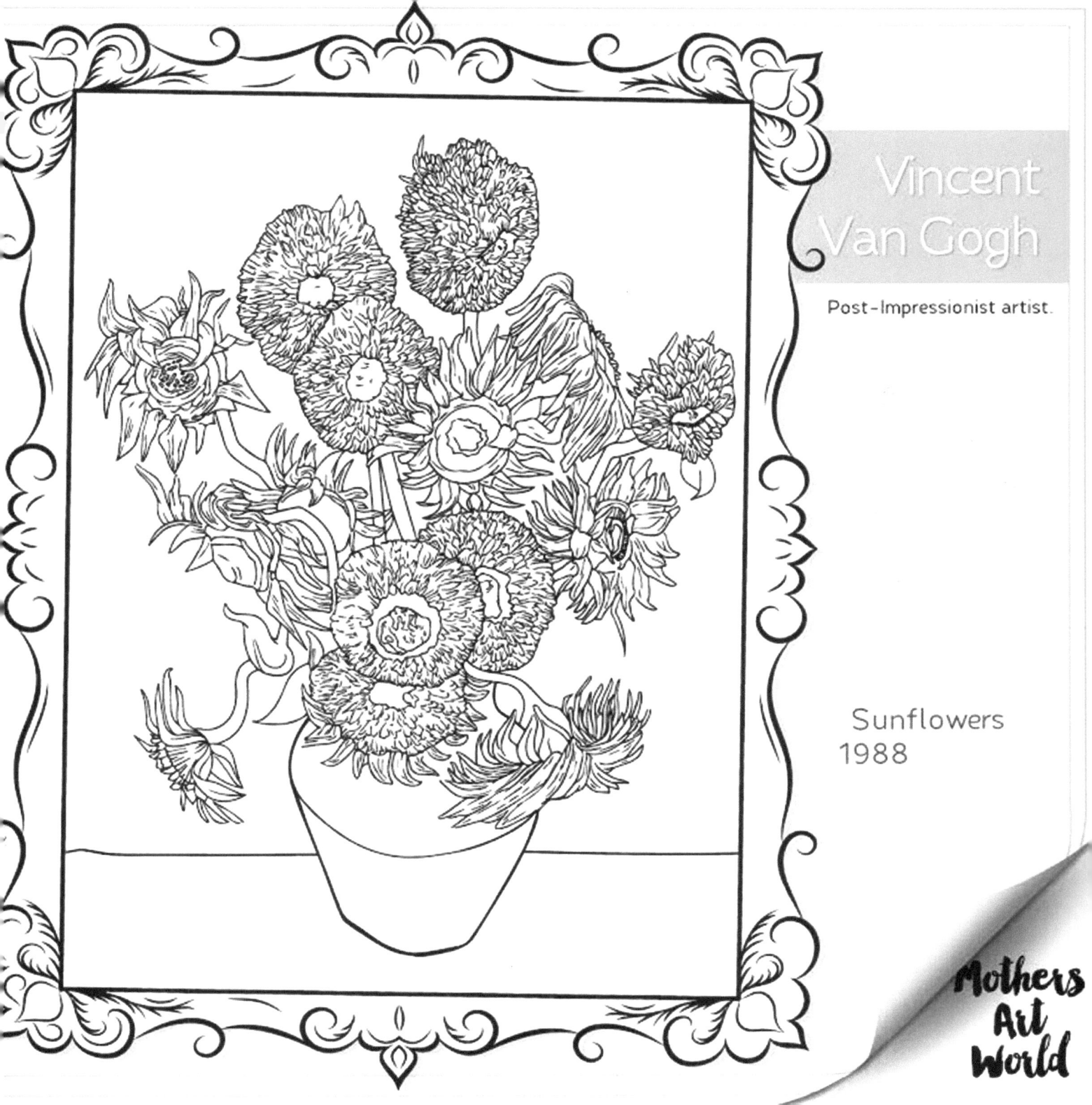

Vincent
Van Gogh

Post-Impressionist artist.

Sunflowers
1988

Mothers
Art
World

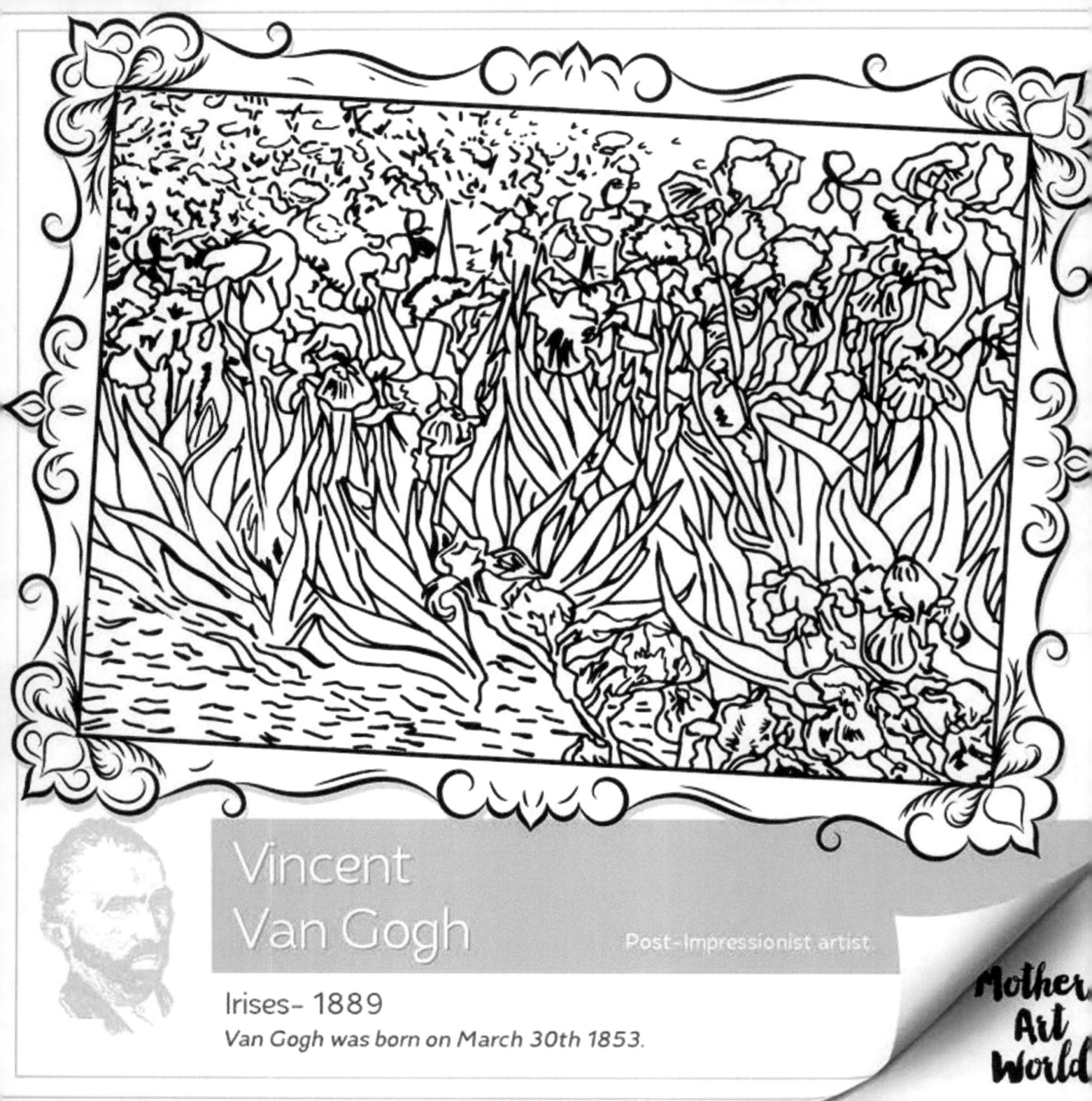

Vincent Van Gogh

Post-Impressionist artist.

Irises- 1889

Van Gogh was born on March 30th 1853.

Mother Art World

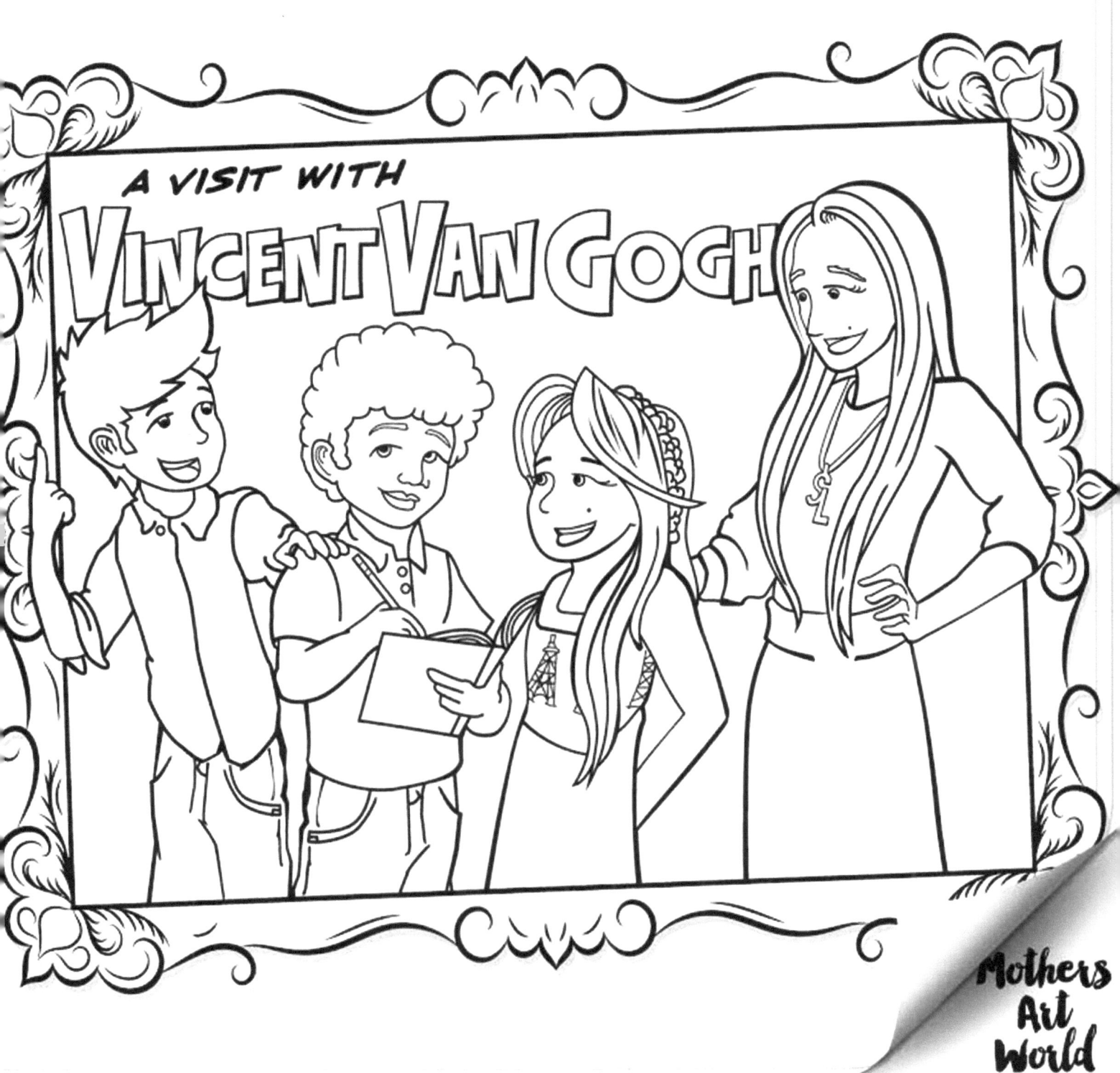

www.ingramcontent.com/pod-product-compliance
Lightning Source LLC
Chambersburg PA
CBHW040747200526
45159CB00023B/1761